ICT TRADING BASICS - The Inner Circle Trader

Understand Key Concepts Such As Market Structure Shift, Institutional Order Flow, Liquidity To Become A Better Trader

Mark M. Darby

All rights reserved. No part of this publication may be reproduced, distributed, or transmitted in any form or by any means, including photocopying, recording, or other electronic or mechanical methods, without the prior written permission of the publisher, except in the case of brief quotations embodied in critical reviews and certain other noncommercial uses permitted by copyright law.

Copyright © Mark M. Darby 2024

TABLE OF CONTENTS

Part 1: Meaning of ICT Trading Strategy...........4
    Inner Circle Trader 4
    Key ICT Concepts 7
    Using ICT Trading Strategy To Predict Price Movements 12
Part 2: Market Structure Shift...........................17
    Market Structure Shift – MSS Explained...17
    Finding Trade Opportunities (Through the Use of Market Structure Shifts)...................21
    Basis of ICT Market Structure Shift...........23
    How to Identify ICT Market Structure Shift 24
Part 3: Institutional Order Flow.......................27
    Effects of Institutional Order Flow 32
Part 4: Liquidity..36
    Market Liquidity...38
    Buy-Side and Sell-Side Liquidity................39
Part 5: Optimal Trade Entry (OTE)..................43
    How to Determine OTE 43

Part 1: Meaning of ICT Trading Strategy

Inner Circle Trader

Market structure analysis is the foundation of the Inner Circle Trader (ICT) Trading Strategy, which is a thorough approach to trading. Its capacity to provide insight into the market behavior of institutional traders is what distinguishes this method. It gives investors the means to avoid the typical traps that come with retail trading, including unanticipated losses, by doing this.

Sound knowledge of market structure is the foundation of the ICT Trading Strategy. When major price movements occur in the financial market, market makers and major participants frequently build up sizable order blocks. In FX trading, where central banks frequently engage in the market, this is particularly true. In the accumulation phase, prices often stay within a corrective range, frequently breaching levels of short-term support and resistance. Still, identifying the exact candle at which the order flow begins is a critical insight that the ICT approach offers.

The functioning of the financial market must also be understood by traders to apply the ICT Trading Strategy successfully. The Asian trading range is the first in its 24-hour cycle of operation. By tracking intraday price sentiment, traders may take advantage of trading opportunities at the best times to profit from this behavior. The London manipulation and the

New York sessions then wrap up this market cycle.

Based on the ICT principle, several trading methods have been created, each with its methodology. It's important to remember, though, that swing trading on a greater time frame and intraday basis is typically more successful than other approaches.

The Inner Circle Trader (ICT) Trading Strategy equips traders with a thorough grasp of the structure of the market, how institutional players affect price movements, and how the market operates as a whole. ICT trading is an approach that uses the actual price movement without depending on several contradictory indications. This trading strategy builds on several ideas to provide a trader with a more comprehensive grasp of the market. Michael Huddleston, a trader, created this ICT trading approach, which is based on the idea of examining market movements via the prism of institutional or "smart money" traders.

- The ICT Trading Strategy is a thorough approach that includes displacements, liquidity zones, market structure research, and other important ideas.

- The strategy's effort to mimic the trading style of institutional market participants, or Smart Money, is one of its standout features.

- Even though the ICT Trading Strategy offers insightful information, a trader's ability to use it in practice relies on their capacity to manage risk well and execute profitable transactions with discipline.

Key ICT Concepts

1. Liquidity

There are two different types of liquidity in the ICT Trading Strategy: buy-side and sell-side. The region of a price chart where stop orders are most likely to be placed by short-selling traders is known as buy-side liquidity. On the other hand, Sell-Side Liquidity pinpoints the areas where stop orders from bullish traders are concentrated.

Buy-Side and Sell-Side liquidity zones are often located at the highest and lowest points of price patterns, which represent the extremes of price volatility. This is because retail traders frequently choose to cancel their holdings in these regions or put stop-loss orders in these locations. The ICT approach relies heavily on liquidity as it aims to mimic Smart Money's trading style, which enables traders to spot changes in the market structure.

2. Displacement

A sharp and abrupt change in price, either upward or downward, is what defines displacement. It usually shows up as a series of successive long candles with short wicks moving in the same direction on a price chart.

According to ICT, displacement usually denotes a quick spike in buying or selling pressure and usually happens when the price hits a liquidity threshold. These are two important things to keep in mind while observing displacement. Furthermore, two important repercussions of displacement are virtually always a shift in the market structure and a gap in fair value.

3. Change in Market Structure

In an uptrend, trends are characterized by higher highs and lower lows, and in a downtrend, by lower highs and lower lows. A level on the chart when the current trend is broken is called a market structure shift. A lower low in an uptrend indicates it, but a greater high is usually reached in a downturn. Usually, a displacement comes before these changes.

Inner Circle Traders use this level as a reference point for transactions and start searching for other signs indicating a change in trend when a price breaches through a Market Structure Shift level.

4. Inducement

At the pinnacles of small-scale counter-trends inside broader trends, inducements are observed.

ICT claims that these moves are frequently the outcome of Smart Money's lower-time frame stop-loss hunting operations.

ICT traders use the theory that the price would revert to its initial trend when an Inducement level is reached and more liquidity has entered the market as the foundation of their methods.

Equitable Difference in Value

ICT traders describe this "gap" on their charts as the moment when a trend reversal happens due to a breach of a liquidity threshold as a fair value gap. With a bigger candle in the middle and a space between its wick and the wicks of the other two candles, Fair Value Gap is specifically made up of three candles.

Why is ICT Strategy So Popular in the Modern Climate?

The ICT trader method has become quite popular since it integrates a lot of helpful ideas in the trading industry. ICT has gathered industry best practices and built a very reliable system, ranging from price actions and trend indicators to stop-loss orders and mirror trading.

ICT flow is quite straightforward, but it requires a high level of technological know-how. Traders must first choose a preferred niche in which to keep an eye on the market and spot any telltale indicators of change.

Using ICT Trading Strategy To Predict Price Movements

There are several settings in the ICT trading technique, ranging from the most straightforward to the most intricate. We will discuss the Liquidity Sweep Strategy, which is among the most straightforward and successful ICT trading setups because trading doesn't have to be difficult.

The interaction between buy-side and sell-side liquidity is the fundamental idea behind the liquidity sweep strategy. A quick liquidity sweep removes sell-side liquidity, which creates the conditions for the price to move in the direction of dominant buy-side liquidity. This in turn frequently sets off a dramatic change in the mood of the market. The Liquidity Sweep Strategy functions more quickly than some other ICT setups, which need to wait for price alleviation or the discovery of supply and demand zones. When legitimate bullish or bearish liquidity sweep patterns are identified in the market, trades are swiftly executed. Let's now examine how this trading strategy operates:

Step 1 Find a Reliable Single Candle Liquidity Sweep Pattern on HTF

Finding a legitimate single candle liquidity sweep pattern on the higher time frame is essential to starting this approach (HTF). This pattern appears as a single candle that sweeps away liquidity under the previous lowest point shortly before a big and abrupt upward advance in a bullish environment. Crucially, the price has to use just one candle body or wick to clear the liquidity below the preceding structure's lowest point.

This pattern's validity depends on the candle that appears following the sweep. It must not close above or below the sweep candle for the setup to be considered acceptable. For a bearish liquidity sweep pattern, the reverse is true.

Step 2: Find a CHoCH by Zooming Into the Lower Time Frame

The next step is to transition to a lower time frame (LTF) and wait patiently for a change in the character pattern (CHoCH) following the liquidity sweep using a single candlestick. This pattern indicates that there has been confirmation of a change in the market structure at the entrance point.

Traders can then proceed to put their limit orders on the newly recognized order block or the fair value gap after receiving this confirmation. The trader has complete control over which of these two entry locations to use. Backtesting may be preferred by some, who may then select the option that best suits their trading style. A hybrid strategy can also be used, with the entry located at the midway of the single zone that represents the fair value gap and order block.

Setting a target profit and stop loss in step three

The stop loss should be placed below the order block when using the Liquidity Sweep Strategy during an upswing. In a downtrend, on the other hand, place the stop loss over the order block. To minimize the effects of any unfavorable slippage, always factor in a spread buffer when calculating your stop loss.

The subsequent opposing swing point in the price action should be the location of the target profit. You may lock in profits when the market goes in your favor and have a clear goal thanks to this.

Based on a thorough analysis of market structure, the Inner Circle Trader (ICT) Trading

Strategy is a complete trading methodology. This method is unique in that it can provide insight into the market behavior of institutional traders.

Part 2: Market Structure Shift

Market Structure Shift – MSS Explained

ICT trading technique is a trading theory based on the analysis of charts and smart money ideas, and one of its main components is the shift in market structure. Technical patterns (or patterns) that indicate a possible reversal in the market's trend are referred to as the Market Structure Shift (MSS) in trading terminology. MSS is a tool used by ICT traders to spot impending stock price reversals and join the market inside the Fair Value Gap which the MSS emphasizes.

Essentially, an MSS is just the moment in time (and on the charts) when the prevailing trend or pattern abruptly shifts, which is the simplest way to explain how one forms one. Practically speaking, though, it may be defined as the point where price spreads over the previous lowest low in a bullish trend or the previous lower high in a bearish trend, respectively, after a series of higher highs and lower lows.

If the Market Structure Shift is verified, ICT traders would often utilize this signal to determine the appropriate area of the chart to establish entry and exit points for their trades. They view this as the first sign of a trend change. After identifying and establishing the current trend, ICT traders must continue to watch the chart in anticipation of a disruption in the status quo, which typically takes the form of a market structure shift.

The moment on the chart wherein the existing trend is broken is referred to by ICT traders as a "market structure shift." To put it another way, it's either the highest point of a higher high that comes after a sequence of lower lows and lower highs, or the lowest point of a lower low following an array of higher highs and higher lows (in a bullish trend).

When a trend change is verified, ICT traders frequently employ a Market Structure Shift as the initial indication and use this chart point as the foundation for their trades.

It is now essential to comprehend the idea of displacing within the framework of the market to completely comprehend MSS. What precisely is displacement, then? It is an abrupt change that is frequently sparked by the arrival of significant competitors. It's an important idea since it helps traders determine their market bias in addition to offering trade entry possibilities. It's also important to remember that traders frequently make the error of detecting an MSS without obvious displacement.

We identify a shift in the market structure during an advance when prices unexpectedly fall below the last low without first hitting a new high. This is a warning sign that a negative reversal may be approaching and that the bullish enthusiasm is waning.

A negative market structure results from traders preparing to sell the asset. However, if the price crosses beyond the latest recent high without falling below the most recent low during a downtrend, this indicates that MSS is present. With buyers now in control over sellers, this break suggests a shift in the sentiment of the market.

Finding Trade Opportunities (Through the Use of Market Structure Shifts)

A downtrend may be recognized by patterns of lower highs and lower lows, or higher highs and higher lows, as we can begin using market structure alterations in trading.

As previously said, when these patterns are disrupted, a market structure shift takes place. For example, a price may signify a possible transition from an upward trend to a downward trend or vice versa when it produces a lower low following a string of higher highs and higher lows.

You may find trading opportunities, predict future market changes, and determine entry and exit locations by recognizing these adjustments. The idea may be used in a variety of periods, providing long-term position traders and short-term day traders with trading possibilities. Keeping that in mind, the following actions are necessary for you to employ Market Structure Shifts in making trades successfully:

1. Determine the market structure currently in place.

2. Keep an eye out for structural flaws

3. Use price action tactics or additional technical analysis instruments and indicators to validate the change.

4. Arrange your transaction.

Basis of ICT Market Structure Shift

The ideas of swing highs, swing lows, and displacement move form the foundation of the ICT market structure shift (MSS). Therefore, you must first understand the ideas mentioned below to comprehend the ICT market structure shift (MSS).

Three candles are arranged in a pattern known as Swing High, with the first and third candles' highs being lower than the second candle's. It is possible to state that the center candle's peak is higher than the peaks of the left and right candles that follow.

A three-candle configuration known as a "Swing Low" occurs when the lows of the first and third candles are higher than the lows of the second. We may conclude that the center candle's low is lower than the lows of the left and right candles that follow.

Moving Away A motion is, in essence, a strong move in one direction. It can be done with one candle or several candles arranged in the same direction.

Large genuine bodies and short wicks are common characteristics of these candles, indicating less dispute amongst buyers and sellers. A fair value gap (FVG) exists between the candles in a displacement with a certain amount of candles.

How to Identify ICT Market Structure Shift

A displacement move combined with a break in the swing high or low indicates an ICT market structure shift (MSS). Bullish or bearish based on the structure of the market Two categories of ICT market structure shifts (MSS) are distinguished below.

A bullish market structure shift occurs when the negative market structure gives way to a positive one. As is common knowledge, prices go lower and reach lower swing highs in a bear market. Bullish market structure shift, thus, occurs when the market swings up with displacement and smashes the lower high, which has previously taken a prior low.

A bearish market structure shift occurs when the bullish market structure gives way to a bearish one. Price swings upward and makes higher swing lows in a bull market, as is well known. A bearish market structure is therefore defined as a market that swings lower with displacement and breaches the higher low (which in turn has previously taken a prior peak).

ICT market structure shift should be used with caution in forex trading since no method is infallible, therefore you shouldn't stake all of your money on it.

In addition, you have to constantly trade with a stop loss set up to safeguard your equity and reduce your dangers.

Part 3: Institutional Order Flow

The term "institutional order flow" in the context of forex refers to the volume of deals that institutional traders execute on the exchange. Professional traders known as institutional traders work for institutions including banks, insurance firms, hedge funds, and pension funds.

Institutional traders can execute deals with extreme accuracy and precision because they have access to a wealth of tools and information. They discover successful trades and swiftly and effectively execute them by utilizing a variety of trading tactics, including order flow analysis, technical analysis, and fundamental analysis.

One important element influencing price changes in the FX market is institutional order flow. The supply and demand dynamics of the market are greatly influenced by the institutional traders' combined buying and selling of huge quantities of currency pairings. As such, the direction and velocity of price fluctuations in the market can be influenced by institutional order flow.

Typically, electronic trading systems like Bloomberg, Reuters, and EBS are used by institutional traders to conduct their deals. Through the interbank foreign exchange market, which these platforms enable institutional traders to access, they can trade currencies at the best rates.

Market, limit, and stop orders are just a few of the order types available to institutional traders.

While limit orders have to be carried out at a predetermined price or above, market orders are carried out at the going rate in the market. By automatically initiating a transaction when a predetermined price level is achieved, stop orders are used to restrict deficits or lock in gains.

Institutional traders take advantage of price swings in the forex market by employing a variety of trading methods. One well-liked tactic is trend following, in which traders purchase or sell currency pairings in response to trends they see in the market. Mean reversion is an additional tactic used by traders to profit on brief price variations from the average prices of the market by purchasing low and selling high.

Order flow analysis is another tool used by institutional traders to find winning deals. To determine regions of support and resistance in the market, order flow analysis examines the amount and trajectory of trades. Traders can set orders to buy or trade currency pairs at these price points in the hopes that the market will reverse or maintain its trend by recognizing these locations.

News and economic data are also used by institutional traders to guide their trading decisions. The employment, inflation, and GDP statistics are examples of economic data that may have a big influence on changes in the price of the currency market. Institutional traders make use of this data to modify their trading plans and seize chances in the market.

What causes the institutional order flow?

Order flow is the quantity of orders that are in the queue at a certain pricing point.

Consider an instance when an asset's price is sharply increasing. But we are aware that this increasing trend will ultimately halt. The rally is the result of a greater number of traders wanting to purchase the asset than those looking to sell it. There are more buyers than sellers as a result, creating a disparity in the market. The price rises as a consequence. The purchasing impulse eventually wanes and the price hits a point at which there are greater numbers of sellers than purchasers. The price starts to decline as a result of this new imbalance, where there are more sellers than buyers.

This straightforward situation may be seen in the market at both the macro and local levels. This fundamental idea determines whether prices move in a range or in the other way. You can comprehend the forces influencing various price levels by analyzing a chart that displays price movement.

Effects of Institutional Order Flow

How important institutional order flow is in determining market trends

The total number of orders or trades placed in the market by institutional traders, sometimes known as the "whales" of the FX market, is referred to as institutional order flow. Knowing this might make it easier for retail traders to identify possible patterns and moves in the market.

In essence, institutional order flow describes how institutional traders' buy and sell orders affect the movement of prices in the FX market. This effect is large since it can cause notable changes in the market. Retail traders may align their trading tactics with the major participants in the market by noting the trajectory of the Institutional Order Flow, which could result in more lucrative transactions.

Since institutional traders' orders frequently dictate the direction of market movements, it is important to comprehend the directional movement of these orders. Because institutional traders possess the capital to make large market movements, their trading actions frequently start new trends or reverse old ones. Retail traders might structure their transactions by expected future market moves by using institutional order flow analysis to uncover signs of such changes.

Now that we have a better understanding of the importance and effects of institutional order flow, it is critical to know how to examine it effectively to develop trading strategies that work.

Examining institutional order flow to determine the best trading tactics

Examining order book data and market depth is necessary to analyze institutional order flow and ascertain the number and direction of market orders that these traders are placing. To detect possible market changes based on Institutional Order Flow, traders might benefit from using tools and indicators that offer an understanding of the market depth and order book data. Early detection of these trends gives traders the chance to set up their trades for success before big moves in the market take place.

To sum up, institutional order flow in the forex market describes the number of deals that institutional traders execute daily. The resources and data that institutional traders have access to allow them to execute transactions with extreme accuracy and precision.

The dynamics of supply and demand in the market are significantly influenced by institutional order flow, which in turn can have an impact on the direction and speed of price fluctuations. Order flow analysis is one of the trading tactics used by institutional traders to find good trades and make money off of price changes in the forex market.

Part 4: Liquidity

The first and maybe most crucial idea in the ICT trading approach is liquidity. Buy-side and sell-side liquidity are the two categories. On the chart, buy-side liquidity denotes a level where short sellers are going to set their stops. The exact reverse is true for sell-side liquidity. On the chart, it denotes a level at which traders with a long bias will set their stops. Since the highest and lowest points of ranges are frequently perceived as places where traders are "proven wrong" and, as a result, will seek to exit their trades, these levels are frequently located near the extremes in both situations.

Traders that are considered to be "smart money" are aware of this and frequently build-up or divide positions close to levels where a large number of stops are located.

The main factor that enables an additional player to completely understand their situation is the sheer number of stops at crucial points. After the level where a lot of stops are put in place and traded through, the price will frequently turn around and move in the other direction, looking for liquidity at the other extreme.

ICT liquidity in the context of Forex trading refers to the ease with which assets may be purchased or sold without significantly changing their price, as well as the presence of buyers and sellers in the market. Many players in the market due to high ICT liquidity make it simpler to conduct transactions without affecting the price of the market. Liquidity has a significant impact on trading costs and the convenience of entering and leaving positions, thus Forex traders must take this into account.

Market Liquidity

The degree to which assets may be purchased and sold at steady, transparent prices on a market—like the stock market of a nation or the real estate market of a city—is referred to as market liquidity. In the aforementioned scenario, there is no market for refrigerators in return for rare books since it is so illiquid.

Higher market liquidity, however, is what distinguishes the stock market. The price that a buyer proposes for each share (the bid price) plus the price that a seller is ready to take (the asking price) will likely be very close to each other if an exchange has a significant volume of activity that isn't largely driven by selling.

Consequently, investors won't have to forfeit unrealized gains in exchange for a speedy sell. A market is more liquid when the difference between the ask and bid prices narrows; when it widens, the market becomes more illiquid. Compared to stock markets, real estate markets are often significantly less liquid. The size and number of open exchanges on which other assets may be exchanged determine the liquidity of those markets. Examples of these assets include derivatives, contracts, currencies, and commodities.

Buy-Side and Sell-Side Liquidity

What is liquidity on the buy and sell sides?

The ICT trading approach places a high priority on liquidity, which is divided between buy-side and sell-side liquidity. The former is a common stop-order placement location for short sellers on the trading chart. On the other hand, sell-side liquidity indicates a location on the chart where traders holding long positions typically place their stop orders.

These levels are often seen close to the upper and lower bounds of trading ranges, which are places where traders may accept that their transactions were misjudged and want to get out.

Participants in "smart money" actively amass or distribute positions close to locations where stop orders are prevalent, so leveraging such levels effectively. Larger traders can execute their positions more profitably because of the strategy's emphasis on stop orders that are highly concentrated at critical levels. Upon breaching a level that is rife with stop orders, the price frequently reverses course and moves in the opposite direction, chasing liquidity at the opposite extreme.

Buy-side and sell-side liquidity are the two types of liquidity.

The Buy-Side Liquidity is the region on the chart where traders who engage in short sales are inclined to position their stop orders. However, the reverse is also true for sell-side liquidity, which indicates a region where stop orders from bullish traders are concentrated.

Since this is often where most retail traders put their stop-loss orders or choose to liquidate their positions, both the buy-side and sell-side liquidity are typically located in the extremes of price volatility ranges, or near the peaks and depths of price patterns.

The liquidity idea is the most important component of the ICT technique as it aims to replicate the trading behavior of smart money, maybe more so than the other components. Order fulfillment is more likely for Smart Money when they position their orders at levels where a large number of Retail Traders' stop-loss orders are in place. It also provides ICT traders with a glimpse into the future trends as they can forecast what Smart Money will do next.

Part 5: Optimal Trade Entry (OTE)

What is Optimal Trade Entry (OTE)

Determining the perfect or optimal point of entrance into a trading position is known as optimal trade entry, or OTE. This entails carefully selecting the entry point to reduce risk and maximize possible rewards on the deal. OTE is a step in a process that also involves interpreting trading signals and carrying out trading strategies.

How to Determine OTE

The following criteria may be used to determine OTE:

Price Movement Analysis:

Price movement analysis is typically the first step in OTE. Determining potential levels of support and resistance, assessing historical price movements on charts, and understanding the direction of the price all contribute to figuring out OTE. When price approaches or violates a certain support or resistance level, for instance, there can be a chance for OTE.

Analysis of price activity plays a crucial role in figuring out OTE. This analysis entails looking at previous movements in prices on the price chart, figuring out possible levels of support and resistance, and figuring out the overall trend of the price.

- For instance, price swings may present an opportunity for OTE when they occur when the price reaches a particular support level or breaches the resistance level.

Technical Indicators:

OTE may be calculated with the use of popular trading technical indicators. For instance, one may assess the velocity of price movement and probable reversal points using indicators like moving averages, the RSI (Relative Strength Index), and the MACD (Moving Average Convergence/Divergence).

For instance, discrepancies between price movement and the MACD might be a sign of an impending price reversal and should be included when calculating the OTE.

Price Formations:

Price trends are a significant factor in figuring out OTE. Specifically, patterns like inverted head & shoulders, double bottom, or double top may be utilized to determine the OTE as well as signal price turning moments.

When calculating OTE, price formations have a significant role. The utilization of patterns like reverse head & shoulders, double bottom, or double top helps to pinpoint trend shifts and price turning points. For instance, if the price chart displays an inverted head-and-shoulder pattern and breaches the neckline, this may be a good time to purchase OTE.

Events and News:

OTE can also be affected by fundamental and news issues. Important economic data, decisions made by central banks, and political developments are examples of factors that might create abrupt shifts in price movements and could be included when calculating the OTE.

- For instance, a central bank's decision to raise or lower interest rates may come as a surprise and generate a significant amount of market price movement. This can also have a significant impact on the OTE.

The goals of the trading plan, risk tolerance, and trading strategy should all be taken into account while calculating OTE. Finding the OTE is a crucial first step in boosting the chances of a successful trade, but as every trader's circumstances are different, the procedure of figuring out the OTE should always be customized to the trader's particular circumstances.

www.ingramcontent.com/pod-product-compliance
Lightning Source LLC
Chambersburg PA
CBHW070948220526
45471CB00007B/2942